Trial of Jane Leigh Perrot

At Taunton Assizes, on Saturday the 29th day of March, 1800;
charged with stealing a card of lace, in the shop of Elizabeth
Gregory, haberdasher & milliner, of the city of Bath

Jane Cholmeley Leigh Perrot

Alpha Editions

This edition published in 2024

ISBN : 9789362099129

Design and Setting By
Alpha Editions
www.alphaedis.com
Email - info@alphaedis.com

Contents

TRIAL OF JANE LEIGH PERROT.

About half past Seven o'Clock, the Prifoner, attended by a number of Ladies, walked from their Lodgings at the London-Inn, in two or three different Parties, to the Affize Hall, where they waited in the anti-room to the Grand Jury Room, till the Judge came, about Eight o'Clock. She then went into the Prifoners Pen, accompanied by her Hufband and feveral ladies. Mrs. Leigh Perrot appeared very pale and emaciated, between 50 and 60 Years of Age. She was dreffed in a very light lead-colour Peliffe, a Muflin Handkerchief on her Neck, with a Cambric Cravat; her hair of a dark brown, curled on her Forehead; a fmall black bonnet, round which was a purple ribbon, and over it a black lace veil, which was thrown up over her head; while the Jury was called and fworn, fhe appeared perfectly calm and collected, converfing with her Counfel and Friends.——The Indictment confifted of four Counts, varying the owner of the Property charged to have been ftolen. Her Counsel requefted fhe might be allowed a chair, which was granted.

THE PROSECUTION HAVING BEEN OPENED BY Mr. BURROUGH, ... Mr. GIBBS STATED THE CASE FOR THE PROSECUTION.

THAT on the 8th of August, the lady at the bar came to the shop of Elizabeth Gregory, the prosecutrix, in Bath-Street, Bath, where having purchased some black lace, she contrived whilst the shopman Charles Filby, who had been serving her, was gone to procure change of a five pound note she had given him, that she took from a box at the end of the counter, furthest from that at which they had been standing, a card of white lace, that Filby saw her take it, that he would swear it was not by mistake put into the paper parcel of black lace he gave her, that Sarah Raines would confirm him in this; that Elizabeth Gregory seeing the prisoner pass by her shop, in about 20 minutes after, and walking with her husband, went out and accused her of having the lace, that she denied it, but said if it was in the parcel, the shopman must have put it up by mistake, that the parcel was examined and the white lace was found in it; Mr. Leigh Perrott readily told his address; the parcel was not in the state when found in Mrs. Perrott's possession as it had been folded up by Filby for her; and that they, Gregory and Filby, went immediately before the Mayor, to lodge an information, but in consequence of the number of Soldiers who were passing through Bath, for the expedition in Holland, the magistrates could not attend to them 'till the week following.—These were the leading facts of the case, for the prosecution.

ELIZABETH GREGORY, EXAMINED by Mr. BURROUGH.

On the 8th. of August, kept a haberdasher's shop, in Bath-Street, Bath, had an apprentice, named Sarah Raines, a shopwoman, named Leeson, and a journeyman, named Charles Filby, he had liv'd with her about 6 months, at 50 guineas a year; shop, fronts Bath-Street, and as you enter the shop from Bath-Street, on the right hand there is a counter, beyond the counter and at a little distance from it is a desk; on the left hand there is another counter, towards the further part of which, from the door, is a brass railing, upon which goods are sometimes hung; from the entrance to the brass railing, there is about 2 yards and half of counter, and about the same length of railing, at the bottom of the left hand counter is a door, which goes down stairs. On the 8th. of August, Mrs. L. P. came to the shop, between one and two, ask'd to look at the black lace which she had seen the day before, and if the lace expected from town had arrived? Witness said no, shewed her the black lace, which she took down on the counter, at the further end of the brass railing; on the brass railing, veils, shawls and handkerchiefs were exhibited, with which it nearly covered, so that they intercepted the view; at the time witness brought the black lace to Mrs. Leigh Perrott, she was standing at the further end or bottom of the counter, on the outside, and witness on the inside, Mrs. P. fixed on some of the black lace, at that time Filby was at the top, or upper end of the counter, on the left hand side, measuring *white* Lace, they were then taking stock; when Mrs. P. had fixed on the black lace, witness called Filby to measure what was sold her, which he came down the counter to do, he then stood at the bottom of the counter, and in the inside, witness went to the desk, leaving Filby measuring the lace; afterwards she ordered Sarah Raines to clear away the box from counter, which she did, witness sat down at the desk, her face to the counter she had just left, she could see to the end of the shop, and whilst sitting there Filby came for change of a five pound note, given by Mrs. P. in payment of one pound nineteen, for the lace, gave him the change, which he took back to Mrs. P. Witness then went down to dinner, could not say at the time she was going down, where Mrs. P. was, only knows she was gone from the bottom of the counter; little business at that time of the year is done in Bath; no goods were on the right hand counter, nor on the left hand counter, but the veils, &c. on the railing, the box at which Filby had been employed at the upper end, and the box of black lace, taken down for Mrs. P. Sarah Raines at this time was down by the desk, and Miss Leeson was in the shop; Filby shortly afterwards came down stairs, then witness in about ten minutes went back to the shop, saw Mrs. P. pass by the shop in about a quarter of an hour.

At that time she had reason to think lace had been stolen; Mr. P. was with the prisoner on the other side of the street, she went across to them, spoke to her, said, "Pray Ma'am, hav'nt you a card of white lace as well as black?" she said no, I have not a bit of white lace about me; witness said, see in your pocket; Mrs. P. then said, pulling a paper from under her arm, "if I have it, your young man has put it up by mistake;" the paper produced, was not doubled up at the end; Mrs. P. turned red and trembled; witness turned down one of the corners of the paper, and saw the card of white lace, and the black above it; the card of black lace was about an inch shorter, but of the same width; at that time she examin'd the card, and found the shop mark on it, and she said, "It is mine, I will swear that to be the shop mark." On discovering the lace, denied that it had been put up by mistake, and said, "You have stolen it;" this Mrs. L. P. denied; witness took away the white lace. Within half an hour after, went before the magistrates with Filby, but the mayor had left the Town-hall, and no information could be lodged that day; said the Town clerk and deputy mentioned to them the reason of coming, they told her to call the day following, she went, but could not get to the Town-hall, as it was full of soldiers, could not see any of the magistrates; went every day but could only be heard on the Wednesday. Mr. Gye has had the lace one day, since it was taken from Mrs. P. is sure it is the same card of lace now produced.

CROSS-EXAMINED BY Mr. DALLAS.

Has been in that shop two years, succeeded Mrs. Smith, her sister; Smith was in London, carried on the business for her own self, and not for Mr. and Mrs. Smith. When Mrs. P. was in the shop the day before, believes Miss Leeson was in the shop, but does not know who besides. Mrs. P. returned the next day to enquire if the lace expected was come, & then desired to look at others. No customer was there when Mrs. L. P. was served. Filby, when Mrs. L. P. entered the shop was about 5 or 6 yards from the bottom of the counter, when called, came from the top to the bottom to measure the lace; measured it, and made it up in the parcel. The 5*l.* note was given to Filby after the black lace was measured, who was then about 4 yards from witness at the desk. Mrs. P. had on a black cloak, did not know who she was, that is, her name, on either of the days. The best opportunity of taking, is, when many people are in the shop, and some were there. The witness had been examined before the mayor, said then, it was half an hour before Mrs. P. returned by the shop, but cannot now say what time exactly elapsed, between witness going down stairs, and Mrs. L. P. returning to the shop, nor has been able to say this at any time since; no person was present but Mr. and Mrs. L. P. when witness accused the latter. W. Smith is the name still over the shop, notwithstanding an advertisement was in the papers, stating the business to be carried on by Mrs. Smith—it is carried on for the benefit of the witness, Smith's trustees gave the trade over to her, to pay 15*s*. in the pound.

RE-EXAMINED BY MR. BURROUGH.

She has sold goods since that time, has paid debts, and has been answerable for goods, and the 15*s*. in the pound has been paid into the hands of Baron Dimsdale.

Judge Lawrence—"Put in the card of lace."

CHARLES FILBY EXAMINED BY MR. GIBBS.

Lived as shopman with Miss E. Gregory, has been twice a bankrupt, has been with Miss Gregory for 6 months: remembers Mrs. P. coming into the shop on the 8th of August: was at the time, measuring a box of white lace at the upper end of the left-hand counter on the inside, the lace was folded round pale blue cards, which were marked: placed the bottom of the box on his right hand, and the lid on the left: the cards unmeasured were on the cover, those measured, marked and ticketed were put in the box: on the tickets were the quantities measured: when Mrs. P. came in no customer was there: but one person came in for a few minutes only, Miss Gregory was at the bottom of the right-hand counter, Mrs. P. asked if the laces were come from London, Miss G. said no, Mrs. P. then desired to see the lace she had seen the day before, Mrs. P.

looked over part of the laces Miss G. had taken down, and made choice of what she had fixed on the day before: Miss G. called him from the place at which he had been sitting, to measure the laces, which he did: had measured and passed 6 cards of white lace from the lid into the bottom of the box, when he was called by Miss G.—remembers that the last card he had put into the box was very much defaced: did not use the old card but took a new one, and put the shop mark on it: the 6 cards just filled the bottom of the box, the last card was put in the corner of the box, the farthest from the door, was in the act of measuring the seventh when he was called: put the cover with the unmeasured laces on the chair, and on them put the seventh card: measured the black lace Mrs. P. bought: Raines was desired to put the loose black laces into the box, which she did in the inside of the counter, Mrs. P. was on the outside: rolled the bought lace on a small piece of card, some paper was close by, put the lace in it & folded the paper up, (the witness shewed the way with another piece of paper, in which he had folded it) delivered the paper to Mrs. P. who gave him a 5*l.* note for it, which he carried to Gregory to change: had not stirred from the spot on which he stood, 'till he delivered the lace to Mrs. P. and when Gregory had given the change, she went down below; when he received the change from Gregory he turned round and observed that Mrs. P. removed to the other end of the counter, standing with her face down the shop, and the box of white lace on her left hand: passed up to her in the inside, the shawls on the railing first obscured his sight, but when he got up far enough to see her, he saw her left hand come out of the white lace box, with the card of white lace in her hand, which she drew under her cloak; in drawing her hand so quick under her cloak, she rather drew the cloak on one side, which discovered the corner of the card, she had it in her left hand, the card of black lace was in her right: after this Miss G. was down stairs, still Miss Raines & Miss Leeson were in the shop: at that time he did not examine the box of white lace, is certain he saw her take it and under her arm: had conversation with Miss Gregory down stairs afterwards, who came up stairs, he shortly after returned too, he then saw Miss G. with the card of white lace in her hand, which had the private mark he had put on it: he went out and saw Mr. and Mrs. L. P. together, they were apart afterwards, in attempting to speak to Mrs. P. she went to her husband: witness asked his name, said he lived in Paragon-Buildings: witness went to the Town-hall to lay the complaint, but the Magistrates were gone: they were afterwards much occupied with the soldiers who were passing through for the expedition to Holland, attended almost daily till the information was laid.

CROSS-EXAMINED BY MR. BOND.

Smith had left Bath before witness was hired by Mrs. Smith: the goods were the property of E. Gregory, Mrs. Smith was in Cornwall: witness was brought up in the haberdashery line, was a journeyman once in St. Paul's Church-Yard: never had dealings with one Crouch, a pawnbroker: never brought goods to Crouch: was not in the house of Moore and Terry, but was a partner with Terry, who is now gone to Lisbon; they, when together, sent hard-ware to Lisbon, but never himself saw or knew any thing of the goods sent: never look'd into the books, though a partner; their goods sent to Lisbon were bartered for goods; goods were got by them in the City and Birmingham: never dealt with one Caldwell; if Caldwell sent goods through their hands to Lisbon, he knew nothing of it, Mr. Terry alone managed the books, at length they were bankrupts, afterwards became partners with one Crout about 5 months after the said bankruptcy; they were together about 18 months, then this house also was a bankrupt, his certificate is signed yet only by 7 out of 10 creditors; before Christmas there was no name to the certificate, the certificate was never refused by any one; he believes his creditors and commissioners were satisfied, but he believes the solicitor to the commissioners was not: being the confidential servant of the shop, he took the best care he could of every thing: does not know he ever put up in a parcel more things than had been purchased: knows *now* a Miss Blagrave, and recollects when once she purchased a veil at the shop; this happened after Mrs. P's affair, he put up Miss B's veil, Miss B. came back the next morning, and asked if he remembered serving her with a black veil the night before; he said yes, she said you ought to be very careful after Mrs. P's affair, how you do such things; when the veil came back, received it, would not have received the veil if he had not imagined it belonged to the shop: did not tell Miss B. that he had not put up the veil, thinks he told her he did not put it up: knows of no other instance: knows of no person of the name of Kent, who deals in their shop, or any lady who bought gloves in her shop some days before Mrs. P. was there: will say upon his oath that no person complained a few days before that more gloves were put up in a paper than she had bought, very few customers came there at that time, still recollects that nothing of the sort or that any lady cautioned him, but cannot possibly say it did not happen: put the 6th card the left hand corner of the box, and is sure of it, because there was a vacancy in the box when he came to look into it: Miss Raines and Miss Leeson were in such a situation as not to be able to see Mrs. P. is positive Mrs. P. had a cloak on, under which he saw a corner of the card: when he brought back the change Mrs. P. had the black lace in her hand: is positive she did not put the money in her purse: Paragon-Buildings is about a quarter of a mile from the shop: saw her in 20 minutes after it was served; there was time for her to have gone home had she liked it: was in the kitchen about 5 minutes, when he returned he saw Miss G. in the shop, with the card she had taken from Mrs. L. P.

RE-EXAMINED BY MR. GIBBS.

Does not know that he ever put up two veils, or that two were ever put up, knows that a veil was brought back, only one veil was brought back by Miss B; when he went from one end of the counter to the other to measure the black lace, is sure that the card in question, was placed in the box, in the corner; from that time had never been nearer the box, than where he stood to give change, Mrs. P. did not, he is positive, put the change in her purse. The only two persons remaining in the shop, were Sarah Raines, and Miss Leeson, he went up to them, and afterwards down to Miss Gregory.

SARAH RAINES EXAMINED BY Mr. BURROUGH.

She, Miss Leeson, and Miss Gregory were at the bottom of the shop, Filby at the top; when Mrs. P. came, she asked to look at the lace she had seen the day before, this was shewn her; then Raines was desired by Miss Gregory to put the lace away, in which she was employed, whilst Filby was measuring, saw him wrap it up in the paper, and he was in the act of putting it into Mrs. P's hand, when witness went to the bottom of the shop to the desk, to work; remembers Miss Gregory's going down stairs, Filby came to her; Miss Leeson as soon as Mrs. P. went out of the shop, then went down stairs, Miss G. came up first in about 10 minutes, then Filby came up to Miss G. she having returned with lace in her hands; has been in the habit of seeing Filby put up things, he does it carefully, and laces in particular; is positive he only put up the black lace.

CROSS EXAMINED BY Mr. JEKYLL.

She was bound apprentice to Mr. Lambe; Miss G. called her to put away the black lace, which she was employed in all the time she was absent from her work, to this her attention was principally directed, nothing particular led her to attend to putting up the lace; she did not see Mrs. P's purse in her hand, or Mrs. P. put any money into it.

RE-EXAMINED BY Mr. BURROUGH.

Although you were apprenticed to Mr. Lambe you served Miss Gregory always.

EXAMINED BY JUDGE LAWRENCE.

She saw him put only the black lace into the parcel, she is sure of this, she was looking at him.

Mrs. Perrott, being called on for her defence, then spoke.

"As my counsel are not permitted to make any observation on my case, I will say a few words myself. Placed in a situation the most affluent with a supply so ample, that I was left rich, after every wish was gratified, blessed with the affections of the most generous of husbands, what inducement could I have to commit such a crime? depraved indeed must that mind be, that under such circumstances could be capable of it; you will hear from my noble and truly respectable friends, what has been my conduct and character for many years; you will hear what has been and still is their opinion of me, can you suppose that disposition so totally altered, as to lose all recollection of the situation held in society, to hazard for this meanness, my welfare and reputation, or to endanger the health and peace of a husband I would die for; you have heard their evidence against me, I shall make no comments upon it, I shall leave that task where I am confident it will be exercised with justice & mercy, I know my own oath is inadmissable, but I call that God, whom we all acknowledge and adore, to attest that I am innocent, and may he or you punish me, as I speak truth or false in denying it, call that God to witness, that I did not know I had that lace in my possession, nor did I know it, when Miss Gregory accosted me in the Street; I have nothing more to say."

JOHN CROUT, EXAMINED BY MR. BOND.

Knows Filby & his brother, he has more than once or twice done business at Crout's house, supposes he was a haberdasher.

CROSS EXAMINED, BY MR. GIBBS.

Has seen him, and had dealings with him, since 1793, Charles Filby might not have been more than once or twice.

MISS BLAGRAVE, EXAMINED BY MR. DALLAS.

Was at Bath in August last, in September went to Gregory's shop to buy a veil, the 19th. of September, she bought the veil from Filby, she went home, and on opening the parcel, she found two in the said parcel, next day she went to the shop to return the veil, she asked him if he recollected she bought the veil the day before, he said yes, she told him he had put up two, he said he was obliged to her, but he had not missed it.

CROSS-EXAMINED, BY MR. GIBBS.

Was not acquainted with Mrs. P. till she came here, she carried back the veil the next morning, when he said he was obliged to her, but she had never been accus'd by the people of the shop, for taking it.

MARY KENT, EXAMINED BY MR. JEKYLL.

Resides sometimes in Bath, went in August last to Gregory's shop, about the beginning, bought 4 pair gloves, she believes Mrs. Smith's sister serv'd her, they were put in a parcel, she carried them home, on opening the parcel, she found 5 instead of 4 pair, she returned to the shop the next day, she saw Filby, but had nothing to do with him.

GEORGE VANSITTART, ESQ. Examined by Mr. PELL. MEMBER FOR BERKSHIRE.

Has known Mrs. P. 24 years, having the greater part of that time, lived in Mrs. P's neighbourhood, from all I saw or heard of her conduct and character during that time, I conceiv'd her to be a person of honorable and religious principles, incapable of an act of dishonesty; Mr. P. is a man of fortune.

LORD BRAYBROOKE, EXAMINED BY MR. BOND.

Has been acquainted with Mrs. P. 34 years, I always considered Mrs. Perrott's character to be most honorable and unimpeachable, I know no family in the neighbourhood whose character stood higher.

MR. ANNESLY, EXAMINED BY MR. DALLAS. MEMBER FOR READING.

Have been acquainted with Mrs. P. 30 years her general character was most respectable, she was beloved by her neighbours, and no one could have any suspicion she would ever do any thing dishonorable.

JOHN GRANT, EXAMINED BY MR. JEKYLL.

He has known her 26 years, she bore a most remarkable good character, and they were look'd upon in the neighbourhood as the most affectionate pair in it, and I really conceive there was not a neighbour in all that country, who could have any suspicion that she was capable of doing a dishonorable action; they had an ample fortune.

MR. WISE, EXAMINED BY MR. PELL.

Vicar of Wargrave has known them 17 years, I have had frequent opportunities of seeing Mrs. P.—no people ever attended church more punctual; I always believed her a most respectable woman, and that she and Mr. P. were an example to the parish of moral & religious duties, and by no means capable of being guilty of any dishonest action.

Rev. Mr. WAKE, EXAMINED BY Mr. BOND.

I am curate of the parish in which they live at Bath, have been acquainted with them 8 or 9 years, from the time I became curate I have been pleased and surprized at their constant attendance at church, and have always admired the religious habits and conversation of Mrs. P.—if I had been desired to name a person capable of a deed so foul as that imputed to Mrs. L. P. she would have been the last person.

WINTHORPE BALDWIN, ESQ. EXAMINED BY Mr. DALLAS.

I have been well acquainted with both several years, I have always heard the best of characters of her, as most affectionate to her husband, free from levity, vanity and extravagance, and incapable of committing a crime of this sort.

W. H. WINSTONE, ESQ. EXAMIN'D by Mr. JEKYL.

I have known Mrs. Leigh Perrott five years, she always has appeared a woman of the highest honour, and the last person I should suspect of an accusation of this kind.

Dr. MAPLETON, EXAMINED BY Mr. PELL.

I have known her near 30 years, she has always been a most respectable character, I, as well as numbers of my friends have known her to be such.

Mrs. WINSTONE, EXAMINED BY Mr. BOND.

I have known her 4 or 5 years; I know not a more respectable woman, & if I had not thought so, I should not have appeared here in this public manner. *NOTE.—Mrs. W. was at the bar with the prisoner.*

Miss CHOLMONDELEY, EXAMINED BY Mr. DALLAS.

I have known her 40 years, she is a person who has always borne the most respectable character for religion, and in every other respect: I have been in great intimacy with her.

Mr. T. COWARD, EXAMINED BY Mr. JEKYLL.

I am a linen draper, and live at Bath; have known her 8 or 10 years, have always thought her a woman of the strictest honor, she has been a customer of mine, and I have never had a doubt of her honesty.

W. LONSDALE, EXAMINED BY Mr. PELL.

I live at Bath and am a silk-mercer, I have known her 4 years, she is a woman of the highest honor.

Mr. WRIGHT, EXAMINED BY Mr. BOND.

I am a jeweller and perfumer at Bath, have known her 5 years, have had the highest opinion of her, she is very honest and very strict.

JUDGE LAWRENCE went through the evidence most ably, in the course of which he observed that the character given her was the very best; that if the Jury had any doubt, her character ought to weigh in her favor, but that this would depend on their consideration of the facts; that if they believed Filby, they must pronounce her guilty, for the facts he had stated proved the offence, but that still there was a material fact in her favor, the circumstance of her returning to Bath-Street so soon, when she might have gone home and concealed the lace; the case however was left with them.

The Jury deliberated near half an hour, and returned a verdict of NOT GUILTY.

FINIS.

Milton Keynes UK
Ingram Content Group UK Ltd.
UKHW030744071024
449371UK00006B/557